Business Corner: What's Really Needed to Survive the Entrepreneurial Fight

By: J Haleem

Limits of Liability and Disclaimer of Warranty

The author and publisher shall not be liable for your misuse of this material. This book is strictly for informational and educational purposes.

Warning – Disclaimer

The purpose of this book is to educate and entertain. The author and/or publisher do not guarantee that anyone following these techniques, suggestions, tips, ideas, or strategies will become successful. The author and/or publisher shall have neither liability nor responsibility to anyone concerning any loss or damage caused, or alleged to be caused, directly or indirectly by the information contained in this book.

Table of Contents

Dedication

I dedicate this book, *Business Corner: What's Really Needed to Survive the Entrepreneurial Fight,* to my Uncle Latif. He was always in my corner. Growing up as a kid, I didn't recognize this. He was the only one of my family members that kept a consistent job. He was the first person I saw in my family tell their wife she didn't have to work. He worked while she stayed home. I remember that she didn't know how to cook, so he bought her cookbooks, lots of baking dishes, and pots and pans for her to experiment and learn how to take care of the family.

It was at his house that I first saw someone have a washer and dryer in their home. It was at his house when I was able to go and sleep in a bed on my own as opposed to on a couch or sharing a bed with any one of my cousins or siblings.

This was always special. He was there during one of my life's most important events. If you know my story, then you know when I was young, I turned to the streets to make money. At 14 years old, I got shot. My grandmother, who had custody of me wasn't around; she was in South Carolina at her dad's funeral. I stayed with Uncle Latif the entire time.

He cared for me, and made sure I was good, and that I was safe. He never once had a conversation where he was judging me and saying you have to get your life together. He understood I had to do what I had to do. Instead, he'd say, *"Be careful nephew. You gotta watch yourself out there nephew."* Knowing where he had come from being released from jail six years prior, he understood. He saw where I was going and I didn't stop after that. I got into selling drugs a lot more after I had recovered. Not one time did he ever tell me anything negative, or cursed me for doing so.

He always provided support. His house was the house I was able to go to and not be in the place where I did my dirt. His house is where I was able to go and still feel safe, comfortable, leave my money on the table, and not worry about nobody stealing it. He still provided me with everything that I needed and the support that I needed from a man at that time. I only wish before he passed away that I was able to realize this and recognize him for being that strong tower that I didn't know I needed, and didn't acknowledge at the time.

He knew how I felt about him. My whole family knows how I feel about him. And I know how he felt about me before he left this world. I want to take the time in this book to honor and dedicate this book to him because in my life he was a continuous support system. I knew that he would've loved to see me where I am today. He still would've been supporting, he still would've been cheerleading, and being my own personal Amen Corner.

I feel like we lost him too soon, but we always feel that way about our loved ones. But I know that he knows that I'm grateful. I wish I could have told him publicly for everybody else to hear it, but I believe that this book will suffice and make him even more happy and more proud of his nephew.

The point of this book is to teach people how important being supportive is. How important it is not being judgmental, being a support system to your siblings, your friends, your children, and to an entrepreneur, and helping them to be as successful as they can be. We need more people in the world like my Uncle Latif.

Introduction

Nowadays, it seems that being an entrepreneur is the coolest thing in the world. I remember being in college thinking that I wanted to be an entrepreneur. It seems crazy to me now. 20 years ago, I attended an HBCU, and at the time, they were telling most Black kids going to college that this is where you should enroll. Even today families and those in the Black community tell you that's where you're supposed to be because that's where you're going to get the most nurturing. They say that you will be amongst your people. Well, that was me, amongst my people telling them that I want to be a businessman. I had all the call signs.

I lived in South Carolina, but I'm from Newark, New Jersey, right outside of New York City. Sometimes, I would drive 11 and a half hours to get wholesale merchandise. I brought the merchandise all the way back down to South Carolina to sell. These were white t-shirts that I would get for $20 a dozen. I sold them for $5 each and in turn made $60.

I got multiple packs of white t-shirts, and I also would get bootleg movies, and knockoff Gucci and Louis Vuitton purses and sell those as well. I always had a hustle and had something going on. I threw parties and even invested into the restaurant industry with a friend. Even though I was doing this amongst my people, which I believe should have been celebrated. They had a negative reaction and told me that I should get a job.

During my senior year of college, I was talking to a professor of one of my classes. He said that he was in debt up to his eyeballs. This was ironic because his mother died in debt and her last wish for him was to not die like she did. He was preparing to put his first child through college that same year, and he would have to go into college in debt.

This was the inspiration for him telling us about jobs that were available and how important it was to get a job right out of college and pay your bills.

One difference between me and some of my other classmates, is that I was a felon. I said to him, *"I'm not going to be able to get a job."* He said, *"What do you mean? Everybody can get a job."* I said, *"Not me."* I shared with him what I've been through. He said, *"Man, well, if one job doesn't happen, keep applying until you get one."*

I started out with that idea. The first three jobs I applied to were career jobs. They all said no. Well, they said yes, I was hired. I went through all the paperwork processes and completed background checks. I had gone so far as to sign my offer letter and the next thing you know, about a week or two later when my background check came back, they had to resend my offer letter because they found out I was a felon. At that point, I said to myself that I don't want to experience this level of rejection anymore. That was my first time feeling that type of rejection.

However, this is not the rejection that a lot of entrepreneurs get used to feeling. They tell you as an entrepreneur, that you must get used to hearing "No." At that point, I learned no is different depending upon who it comes from. When you're a salesman, and you're selling door-to-door, you get used to hearing the word no. It's a numbers game.

When you went to college, did all you were supposed to do academically, and graduated with good grades, getting a job should have been simple. But when you get hired, and then let go before you start, and it's happened three times in a row; that's a different type of no. Even in entrepreneurship, you don't get those no's.

In entrepreneurship, we start to differentiate those no's when we cross that path. One of the biggest no's that you experience is when you are looking for support, when you're working on a plan or a vision and someone that you love tells you no, they're not going to support you financially or otherwise, or your spouse doesn't claim what you're doing. They separate themselves and say, *"That's their business, not mine."* Or when your friends don't answer your phone calls anymore because you have another new business venture, that's a different type of no.

What starts to happen is that entrepreneurs seek refuge in their business because they realize it's all they have. The success or failure of the business is going to define them, their career, and most importantly, their life. How do they make it out of this position? If you go back to a job, then everybody will say I told you so. You are just like everybody else.

If you crash and burn, then they told you so. If you succeed, then you likely killed yourself in the process. Is it worth it? Ask Mark Zuckerberg, Elon Musk, Byron Allen, or Russell Simmons. Ask all the people you know that may have had a vision. I've named only a few, but you can think of your own examples. I have plenty of other people to name, but the examples I gave are of people who are changing or have changed the world and how we do business.

If they didn't have a vision, then you wouldn't be using their products. You wouldn't be using Facebook, PayPal, listening to Hip Hop Music globally, or being able to see a Black man own a weather channel. In order to create the platform, or merchant payment service, for example, they had to be entrepreneurs.

My answer is yes, it's worth it. It's always worth it to do something everybody else is not willing to do. It's always worth it to change your life for you, the next generation, and the people around you. The problem is we shouldn't have to do it alone. You should have somebody around to support you, to pick you up when you're down, and to hold your arms up like they did for Moses, (Exodus 17:12). If you are the visionary, then you must have somebody with you to help carry that vision.

I decided to write, *Business Corner: What's Really Needed to Survive the Entrepreneurial Fight* because we have to normalize supporting entrepreneurs. We must normalize supporting visionaries, those people who are going to change the world, and are willing to do what we don't have the guts to. We must normalize that. We must make it easier and simpler for them to go ahead and do the great work they were put here to do.

The visionary that's willing to create the town that you are comfortable living in, support them. The entrepreneur that has the vision for the grocery store you will be shopping in, support them, especially if you are not willing to figure out how you are going to create your own. If you're not willing to support them, get out of their way.

I don't have to continue to tell you how hard it is to be an entrepreneur. I believe that half of you reading this book, don't even want to be entrepreneurs because you know how hard being an entrepreneur is. You had a front row seat watching people fail. This is the point of the book. These entrepreneurs wouldn't have failed if they had help. They wouldn't have succumbed to their issues if they had help. Everybody experiences challenges in life and business, but those challenges are easier to handle when you have somebody in your corner.

Business Corner is here for that entrepreneur who feels as if they're alone. Who feels as if they've been forgotten about, and that everybody's standing on the sideline, watching and waiting to see them fail. We will no longer be able to be bystanders in this community. *Business Corner* is designed to help hold those individuals accountable.

Maybe you don't know how to help the entrepreneur, who's your spouse, your son, or your daughter, or your best friend. Maybe you don't know how to deal with your friends and family not helping *you* in this book. I promise that you will find out. Ultimately, you'll discover that you will never be alone again on your entrepreneurial journey because you've read *Business Corner* and I've given you what's really needed to survive the entrepreneurial fight.

Section One:

READY. SET. FIGHT.

DECISION-MAKING

Round 1
Getting the Vision

As you can probably guess, entrepreneurs need the most assistance and support during their idea phase because many businesses are killed during this time. Beautiful visions and ideas are sometimes kicked to the curb once brought to a parent, spouse, or friend. Let's think about the kid that's 14 or 15 years old, who spends all his or her time and energy playing a video game, singing in the mirror, playing basketball, rapping, or fixing up cars.

Maybe they enjoy breaking things and putting them back together. These are all signs that they can be great at their chosen hobby. This is the age where Gary Vaynerchuck says that we know the career we want to do for the rest of our lives.

At the same time, children growing up may have heard their parents say to them that when you grow up, you are going to get a real job. You're going to grow up and do something that's going to make you some guaranteed money so that you will not be poor. Then as we go further and further in life and your children are off to college, and now as an adult, you're telling them about other careers and opportunities.

In my experience, we were being told about all the things we couldn't do, what wouldn't happen, and what wouldn't work. It had to be the way our parents or advisors were telling us to move or else.

And then you get to a point where it becomes your mindset and that's all you're thinking about. You're focusing more on what won't work as opposed to the possibilities of your dreams coming true, and the possibilities of you doing the things you want to do. I often talk about the idea phase as a lonely phase because the idea comes to you and only you. Maybe the idea came to you from something you saw on TV, you dreamed about, or you went to a basketball game, or a concert, or you saw a person playing the piano.

You liked how the stage was set, in particular the stage lighting. Not only did you like the lighting, but you took it a step further and became really interested in it. You saw it as a career. For me it was car dealerships. At a young age, I fell in love with them because I spent a lot of time at the one that was located at the end of my block. It was at this moment that the seed was planted for me to want to work with cars. Now, I am sure this surprises the people who know me because I am known for not wanting to get my hands dirty. However, I always wanted to sell cars.

One trait I always possessed was the gift of gab. They didn't call it that when I was a teenager. They said I talked too much. I later realized that talking too much was a strong suit of mine. It was a superpower. I believe that made me prone to want to own a car dealership. Whenever I mentioned to someone that I was interested in owning my own car dealership, what came back to me is that you're in college, you better get a real job.

Then you graduate college and get married. You and your spouse are loving your life, you both have good jobs, and you're paying the bills. You are going on trips from time-to-time and life is good. What happens next is that you get an idea and you want to start this business. Your spouse says, "Are you serious? I'm not doing that."

Granted you probably have friends you have seen fail at entrepreneurship and your husband or wife is adamant about you two not going down that road. I'll bet you behind the scenes most of the time that business idea tanks from lack of support, lack of resources, and no one to lean on. This is what we want to prevent. And a lot of them start here in the idea phase.

The idea phase is special because the idea usually comes from a vision. The vision is special because not many people receive a vision. You can be in a room with 10 other people and be the only visionary. You may not feel that way at first because you're alone and you don't want to stand out. You don't want to be the oddball in the crowd.

You want your friends, spouse, and loved ones to have the same thoughts that you have so that you can celebrate and walk on this path together. Yet, you don't know what you're being set up for. You received an amazing vision and you want to see the vision come to fruition in your life. As a result, you do what comes naturally. You want to tell somebody.

In the Bible, every time Jesus performed a miracle, He told them not to tell anybody. As soon as the miracle was performed, they couldn't wait to run and tell as many people as they could. That's how it is. When you get a vision, you want to tell somebody because you want someone to share the situation with you, you want to give them the beauty of it.

You want to describe to them, what you saw, how it can be, and how your life can be a lot better. In your excitement, you failed to realize that they didn't see it. Some people will never see it, and it doesn't mean that they don't love you. They just don't have the vision. The vision is yours and yours alone. Regardless of what, if you decide to go down that path, a lot of it will be alone. In the idea phase, it's up to you to make a choice. Do you pursue it no matter who's gonna be on your side? Or do you let it die like the other thousands of ideas that you have received throughout the course of your life?

Round 2
Freedom over Finance

After you make the decision of following your idea and the vision that was given to you, one of the factors that you have to understand as an entrepreneur, is making the choice of freedom over finances. Now. Wait. Wait. Wait. I know everybody on social media is telling you that you're going to make all this money. Making the money is compelling because for all intents and purposes, it's true. The only missing piece is that they don't tell you how long it's going to take.

Because of this, we leave our jobs early thinking to ourselves, that in three to six months, I'll be a millionaire. And it really doesn't work that way. While you may not make the money immediately, what does start to happen, as soon as you leave your job, is that you become free. What I've discovered is that a lot of us are not as comfortable in freedom as we think we are because we get so caught up in our daily routines. Maybe you've been on a job for 10 to 15 years, and when you wake up in the morning with nothing to do, that changes you.

After making this decision, freedom will be the second loneliest portion of your entrepreneurial journey. It becomes that lonely because your income goes down. You're no longer at work with your friends, and your routine changes immediately. This is the part of your entrepreneurial journey where people really can't be in your corner because you're not experiencing any negativity from entrepreneurship. You haven't really dived in yet, but you're still dealing with your decision.

As we all know, especially as adults, that a lot of decisions we make, we have to deal with them alone. When you choose to leave your job, the routine of going to work, seeing the same people, and being invited to certain events, such as happy hours, birthday parties, and kids events, stop almost instantly. In addition to your social life changing, you're no longer making the money that you once made.

This puts you in a tight spot, but this is the time when you're supposed to be in your own corner. This is when your faith steps in. This is when your belief steps in because it will be a lot of second guessing at this point after that first month. You are no longer getting those checks that you were so comfortable with. Your thought process changes. You start to ask yourself, have I made the right decision?

Even the greatest prize fighter has to make the decision to get in the ring. On the walk to the ring, he or she is totally alone. Like the prize fighter, it's only your prayer and belief in God that will get you through. Hell, if you're a believer, this is who gave you the vision in the first place.

Most entrepreneurs, when they leave their job in the first week or two, do nothing because they're used to doing the same thing every day. They don't know how to set up their schedule, and set up their workflow that's already been put in place for them by their job, the big organization or corporation they've been working for. Their daily routine consisted of going to work, doing their job, and coming home.

Until you're forced to, you don't realize how hard it is to break a habit, but it's very hard. They say it only takes 30 days to create a habit. If I had to guess, I would triple or quadruple that to break the habit. Some people may say differently, but when you know habits, you know that that is complete bs. When you leave that job and you decide you want to be an entrepreneur, especially full-time, you're gonna take that break in the beginning.

Your break might not be two weeks, maybe it's only two days, but immediately you're not going to go and have an eight-hour schedule, sit in a commute for an hour, and do all the things that you used to do. You're going to sit around on a couch, watch some tv, eat some of the food that you usually wouldn't eat, and catch up on some of your shows that you normally wouldn't watch. This was not your normal life and that's okay, but now it's your first taste of freedom.

However, we all know that freedom is not free. At some point the work begins, and now it is all on you. There is no one telling you that you have a deadline by this timeframe. You no longer have a supervisor who's making sure you have your quarterly reports or projections together. It's all on you, and once you get over that hump mentally, to know that you're going to have to put the same amount of effort and energy and a lot of times *more* energy into this vision and this idea than you ever did with your job. It is at that point when you can start to become free.

True freedom starts with honesty. That means being honest with ourselves. We have to tell ourselves the truth. We have to tell ourselves this is going to be hard work and that it is going to be mostly an uphill battle. If we fight and do what we are supposed to do, then at the end of that battle, we will get those finances that everybody's talking about. It's funny how they choose to leave out those other details.

As a veteran entrepreneur, I understand it's because people don't want to relive those traumas. They don't want to relive those bad days. People don't want to tell you about the time when they were horrible at their business. They only want to tell you about when they were great. Show me the business owner that shows you all their bad reviews on Google or Yelp, as opposed to showing you thousands of good reviews. They're breaking their neck trying to get those reviews removed or getting more reviews so you don't see those.

This holds true in going from freedom to finance. In entrepreneurship, we are choosing freedom over the finance. For me, when I chose to leave my job, my income immediately went to the bottom. But now, I look back at it and see that I never missed a school function with my children. That's freedom. I never missed a trip with my children. That's freedom. I never missed a doctor's appointment. I never missed anything that was important in my children's life because of the decision that I made as an entrepreneur.

I was always available and ready to do anything that needed to be done for my family. Yes, the finances took a few years to come to where I would feel comfortable, but when it came, it was hot and heavy and there was nothing anybody could do to take it from me. It was nothing anybody could do to make it bad for me.

I was happy that I was able to take the success and still be able to spend the same time with my family, take their life to another level, and still have me there in the process. A lot of people would tell you, in order to have the money, you'll have to be away from your family. You'll have to be away from your spouse. I like to submit to you that that's not true, but you have to be a true entrepreneur. You have to truly choose freedom first.

And as you become free and more free and more free and you actually pay that price, the finances are not too far behind. But you have to be honest with yourself from day one that it's going to take work and it's going to take that level of sacrifice in order to get to the promised land that you saw in your vision.

Round 3
Authenticity

Going into the next phase of your business, it's important that you remain authentic. As I've said many times thus far, you are the only person to get your vision. The best part is that you got this vision being who you are. God, the Universe, Infinite Intelligence or whatever you believe in, didn't give you this vision as someone else. He didn't give you this vision for you to become someone else. The vision was given to you as the person you are. In order to carry out the vision, you have to remain authentic.

For example, think about the thing that made you smile when you saw the place that you were going to be. Your smile came from an authentic place because it came from the place that you were in at the time. Your initial excitement about the money you were going to make, that was the genuine excitement you were going to have. It all came from an authentic space.

Once we get into the entrepreneurial phase of business and we go out and talk about what we are doing, this is when the opinions start. People start telling you exactly what you should do. Even if they didn't help or support you, they will still have an opinion. It may be your spouse, parents, or pseudo mentors that you watch on YouTube.

Maybe it's the people that you looked up to because they were in business, maybe they did the same thing that you're trying to do, and they like to tell you what worked for them. A lot of time what works for them doesn't work for you because it's not authentic. If you're not a person who wears a suit and tie every day, then it might not be the best idea for you to start wearing them everyday now.

In business, more often than not, people buy you before they buy your product or service. That's the first thing. Now, after years and years of being in business, the product or the service stands alone and your customers will then say, *"Okay, we are going to go ahead and support that product or service regardless of whether you are in the room or not."* Once people deal with you, it's hard for them to want to deal with your representative.

For instance. Let's say you're having a technical issue. A lot of us, when we call to troubleshoot a problem, we don't want to get an automated message or have to talk to a computer. When you're trying to solve a problem, you want to talk to a live person. A lot of times we want to talk to the person who sold us on the product or the service.

When you have to talk to a representative, you are already on edge. It's the same situation when a customer is dealing with you. You have to be the person you were, when you sold them a product. You have to be that person they believed in, the person they took a chance on. Remaining authentic in this space means everything because this is the time where you'll start trying new things, or other things such as new sales tactics or marketing strategies.

Regardless of what you try, you have to remain yourself in that process. You have to think about that as you're getting all this new information, becoming a student of YouTube university, and attending seminars. Once you've finished your research and studies, ask yourself how does the information that I'm getting work for me? Not how it worked for Tom, Dick, Susie, and Harry? Ask yourself the following questions, How does it work for me? How does it fit in with me and my lifestyle?

For example, I don't live in New York City. I live in Swamp Fox, Iowa. What works in New York City doesn't work in

Swamp Fox, so how can I use this information to my advantage? If I were in New York, I could put posters of my event on the subway, but because we don't have a subway out here, I can't do that. On the other hand, if you're the person who lives in New York, then you have to internalize, and say, How will this work for me in New York?

Let's use another example. If you are an introvert and not an extrovert, you don't have to become an extrovert in order to sell or do well in your business. You have to only ask yourself, what's the best way for me to operate my business as an introvert? Once again, people are going to buy you, which means they want to see the best you possible.

You doing a horrible rendition of an outgoing salesperson will turn them off as opposed to you setting up a way to get people to come to you. Once they are coming to you, your job then becomes to tell them about your product or your service. That's the difference. This is authenticity. People *will* come to you. You might have to invest some money, and get a booth somewhere and dress it up nice so people can keep coming.

Once you have them there, your job is to tell them about your product or your service as opposed to you going out there and doing cold calls because that's not who you are. It's not your strong suit and that's okay. We have to put a lot of time and energy into making sure that we spend the majority of our time in our business performing the tasks that we are the strongest in versus the weakest.

I believe as entrepreneurs that we feel like we have to get stronger at 50 different things. That's not how business works. You are supposed to get stronger at what you're already strong at, and then you hire other individuals or partner with other individuals that are strong in places where you are weak. If you spent the majority of your time trying to become somebody else, getting their skills, gaining their knowledge and talents, then you are never going to grow and be an amazing individual because you are becoming a jack of all trades. You don't have a level of mastery.

Now, sometimes being a jack of all trades is great, especially if you're in a space of survival. If you're trying to survive and you know how to do more than one thing, then yeah, you'll be a perfect candidate for somebody who's going to be able to survive in this world.

Those who desire to reach a level of mastery put in their 10,000 hours and are able to ensure that they will always be able to earn a living. They will always be able to do the things that they need to do for their family, and continue to grow every year. Those watching will see them go higher and higher because they know beyond knowing that they're gifted and have achieved a level of mastery in their chosen craft.

A lot of times once people start talking in our ears or we're trying to save a dollar, we don't want to invest in ourselves, which we will touch on later in this book. We put ourselves in position to try and learn how to do everything and more important, learn how to be like other individuals and get *their* level of success when there's enough success out there for all of us.

There will come a time when we will not only have to go ahead and search for our level of success, but also identify what it looks like in our book of life. Once we identify what success looks like, that's when we'll be able to be our most authentic selves. That's when I believe that we'll be able to triumph in your corner. You need other individuals at this point. You need real friends. You need a wife or a spouse who's willing to tell you the truth, and not tell you what they want to tell you to get the outlook or the outcome that they want.

You need people who are dug in enough to say, *"You know what? I might not agree with this business, or, I don't want to be a part of it, but I'm not going to allow you to be something that you're not, in order to have a business or to do anything."* Those are the people you need to be in your corner at that time because of what you have to sacrifice.

You're sacrificing who you are. You're sacrificing your integrity. You are making a clown of yourself to make a buck. You need people in your corner at that time, people that you know without a doubt are on your team, in your fab five, or tribe. You need the people who are willing to be honest with you during this authenticity phase of your journey to make sure that you don't go out too far on a limb and become something other than who you are supposed to be.

You can find those people, if you don't already have them around you. You need those people around you right now in this phase of your business and keep them around. Those are the people you come back to and say, *Hey, this is what I'm thinking about doing.* Because you know they're gonna tell you the truth, not because they're going to try to manipulate you. Not because they're going to tell you what's best for them or how they want to see you, but they actually are willing to tell you the truth and they don't care that you are going to be upset with them. As you move along on your journey, make sure you have these people in your life as

you remain on your quest for
authenticity.

Round 4
No Plan B

The number one reason for you to become an entrepreneur is freedom, not survival. Nobody should become an entrepreneur only to survive. Once you understand this point and understand what a plan B is, a lot of people especially in entrepreneurship, would run for the hills. They would head for cover because what they're telling you is that your business is going to potentially fail. Whatever you have lined up, if you're focused on a job while you're starting a business, then you're going to have a hard time on that business. It's hard enough when you start a business and have a job. And I'm not discouraging you from having a job.

My point is that your business is going to require pretty much all you have. You're going to be thinking about your business in your sleep. You're going to be thinking about it when you wake up. You're going to be thinking about it when you're out to dinner. However, in this time and in this season, nothing outside of your family should be more important.

Because your family is more important, there should not be a plan B. In these days and times, people like to use the phrase contingency plan. By definition, a contingency plan, is a plan designed to take a possible future event or circumstance into account, (Merriam-Webster, 2022). Let's dive deeper into this meaning.

A contingency plan does not mean that you do something else. A contingency plan is there just in case something goes wrong. This is what they are referring to. However, this doesn't mean that you have to stop your business. Fail safes are put in place so that your business can jump over those hurdles. You don't switch up cars because you're going to go over bumps in the road.

What happens next is that you drive differently, or you take another route, but you're still in the same car. You're still going to the same place. That's the difference. The contingency is in place because yes, something is going to happen. Something always happens. This is referred to as *Murphy's Law*. Anything that can happen, will happen. The way to plan for Murphy to pull in elderly wisdom is to save for a rainy day because they understood that you were going to have rainy days.

And people getting into business thinking that they're not going to have rainy days are delusional. To drive my point, this does not mean do something else. It doesn't mean give it up. It doesn't mean going in a different direction. Everybody, at some point in their business is going through a hardship or will experience an inconvenience. Think about a time when you were stuck in traffic.

You decided to get on the highway to travel to a specific place and as you went along, you ran into traffic. You may have looked on your right and on your left. You sat there, looked across the highway, and saw all the other cars sitting in traffic to. You say to yourself, it's not just me, I haven't been singled out. You chose to take this direction, this path, not knowing there would be traffic, but you got stuck anyway. It's a choice you made, and while this is a part of your journey, it's not the end of it.

There are a bunch of people that's taking the entrepreneurial path that's stuck in proverbial traffic or they're going through their hardships. Remember, you're not alone. What you may not have noticed when you were in traffic, is the car to the right, had somebody with their arms in the air, rocking back and forth, jamming to the music. When you looked to the left, you see someone else sitting in the car with their wife and kids, laughing, and having a good time.

Guess what? They are *all* stuck in traffic. What is it about you? What is it about your journey that's so hard? What is it about your experience that separates you from everyone else? Why aren't you smiling while sitting in the car? Who's with you on this ride? Why aren't you guys enjoying each other? Who's in your corner?

What is it about your journey where you feel like you can't be happy on the path to financial freedom and entrepreneurial success? Is it because of who you have in your corner or lack thereof? Is it because you're frustrated because you're trying to find another way out and you can't? You too can have that same level of success, but you are shooting yourself in the foot from the beginning when you start with a Plan B.

There is no Plan B when you're starting a business. We have to be clear on that. When you get to the point of thinking you have to have a Plan B, reach out to the people in your corner, and solicit the conversation of *seasoned* business owners. Start talking to people who have the testimony of, I've been through hell in my business and now I'm on the other side. You might not know it, but you need to also solicit the help of individuals who have been through hell, used a Plan B and failed. This will help you to gain a balanced perspective.

A lot of people are going to tell you not to talk to people who didn't successfully do what you're trying to do. I think that's total BS. The reason why is because they know more about failure than the other person will ever know, and they can give you tips on how to prevent yourself from going through those pitfalls easier than somebody whose had nothing but success.

Many business owners started their business journey on the job. They stayed on their job the entire time throughout their business. A person on the job running the business doesn't have the same knowledge or experience as somebody who is running the business from scratch with no job, no security, no family giving them any start-up money, or no business loan. Therefore, it is important to surround yourself with people who went through it from the bottom and failed, *and* the people who went through it from the bottom and won.

I have found that these people are not bitter and they have love in their heart. They want to tell you how to do it better than they did. And the person who came from the bottom and won are probably already telling people how to do that. Put yourself in position to be right there in line to get the information that's going to help you. Glean as much information from them as you can. I would advise you to consider taking them to lunch or Pay for their trainings or coaching sessions if they offer them.

Put yourself around them because they are the ones that is going to give you the blueprint to not turn away and not turn back. They're going to make it a little bit easier for you than it was for them. It is because they know that this is a portion of your journey that you do not need to leave up to chance and deal with on your own. Someone else is always going to be doing something more attractive to you at the time.

What you are seeing is the highlight reel and it's going to look very good for you to go on that side and try this and when that doesn't work go on the other side and try what the next person is doing. Again, it's not your journey and that's not the path you need to take to get to the destination that was lain before you. You have the path, whatever traffic comes, whatever bumpy roads you will have to ride on, and whatever messed up bridges you will have to cross, that's your path. It adds to your testimony and ultimately for the success you want to have. A success you would never enjoy if you focused on having a Plan B.

Round 5
It's Time to Resign

One of the hardest times on the entrepreneurial journey that you are ever going to face is the moment you decide you want to leave your job. In the previous chapter, we discussed the No Plan B Theory. This chapter will put you in position to directly act on it. I want you to know that there will be moments when you will be scrutinized more than you have ever been in your beginning phases. And maybe more than you ever will be, except in the case of if you have to file for bankruptcy. In that case, it won't be scrutiny. It would be more like a bunch of, *I told you so's*.

The truth of the matter is a lot less people filed for bankruptcy than they would like us to believe, and a lot less people fail in business, than they would like for us to believe. As a society, we've been conditioned to look at things differently than what they are. How? I'm glad you asked.

A lot of times you trade in your cushy $60,000 salary for a $40,000 business. I can imagine when you went out on your own as a self-employed individual and made $40,000, the people around you would tell you that you're not smart. The person that's making $60,000 a year on a job when taxes are taken out, they're probably going to be bringing home about $40,000 anyway, but no one tells you that. This is why being an entrepreneur works out better financially. The entrepreneur making $60,000 is able to keep the $60,000 putting them in position to get a lot more done.

Another example of something else you would be asked about is how are you going to pay for health insurance? In the Golden Ages, 20 or 30 years ago, I remember when jobs would provide health insurance coverage for their employees. Nowadays, employers will still provide the health insurance, but it comes out of the employee's paycheck. I've heard this specifically in the Black community, but it may be the case in other communities as well.

As a Black man, I've heard it a tremendous amount of times that they will take it out of my check. It's the old adage, *"I won't miss it if I don't see it."* You mean to tell me you're not looking at your check stub and seeing the $400 or $500 being deducted from your paycheck every two weeks? Maybe I'm different, but I notice that type of thing because I know what I can do with that extra money.

As an entrepreneur, you're still doing the same thing, paying for your own insurance, which means you can walk into Blue Cross and Blue Shield and have a conversation with a representative and come out of there with a $1,000/month bill to pay for insurance for you and your family. However, we've been conditioned enough to fight, kick, scratch and crawl, lose friendships and families over the thought that the only sense of security you'll ever have in this life, is having a job.

When you decide to tell your friends and family that you're leaving your job for your business idea or vision, be prepared for the worst amount of scrutiny you've ever had in your life. Also, leaving your job is when you're going to directly have that opportunity to see how many people decide to write you off immediately. The ones who have told you that they love you will write you off. The ones who've told you how much you mean to them, will write you off.

Not only will they write you off, but everything that they ever felt negatively about you will come out. You might not hear it directly from them, but you are going to hear it. Some people are bold enough to tell you to your face, but then with others, you will hear it through the grapevine. Or, you'll hear it through another family member.

This is when your plan B theory will be tested the most because you'll start to get e-mails about job listings. They will bring up jobs, or they will tell you how "so and so" is doing great in their new job or the fact that they recently got a promotion on their job. The same job that you had when you were there.

All the people who purchased from you while you were at work, no longer knows your number to buy your product or solicit your service. You find yourself once again, all alone. This is the time when you will have to lean on those individuals that I talked about in the previous chapter. The people who left their job and started their business and succeeded are the only ones that understand what it is you're going through. They are the only ones that understand and get it. They understand why you felt like you had to make that decision to go into full-time entrepreneurship.

The truth of the matter is a lot of times people go into it with their best intentions, doing everything they are supposed to do, including saving money. Think about the times we are living in now, specifically through *The Global Pandemic*. Thousands of people started their businesses January 2020, only to be met with COVID-19, and a global world shutdown two months later. Outside of the Pandemic, what about the business owner, who experienced a serious health issue?

Each of the individuals mentioned before, started off great - started off how they were supposed to, and yet they were met with circumstances out of their control. This doesn't matter to the naysayers. In their eyes, you should have stayed at your job, although, the same thing that affected your business, affected an individual's capability of maintaining their employment. In fact, it created what we are living through now, *The Entrepreneur Revolution*, which further exposed the uncertainty of the job market as a whole, at least in the United States.

Let's dive into another example. I know a story of a family who had saved for at least three years. They were both gainfully employed and chose to live off one of their incomes. They used the other income to start their business. It was started originally in Germany, and then they moved back to the US.

Through the matriculation of their business, they maxed out their savings, including both of their 401ks. They finally became millionaires once their parents allowed them to use the money from *their* 401ks. Now, trust me, this is not everybody's story. This is not a story that happens on a regular basis. In spite of the challenges, they're filthy rich today because it was one of the family members, one of the spouse's family members who saw the vision, and always supported what they were doing in their business.

Now for a time, the other spouse's family cut them off and the rest of their family did as well. It didn't matter who cut them off, this couple never deviated from their plan *and* they always had somebody in their corner. They didn't start with a contingency plan, or a plan B. Their contingency plan was to pull in more money. The bigger the risk they took, the greater the reward was that they experienced. I have to say it again. Most of the time those who start out in entrepreneurship, do not have this experience. There will have to be sacrifices and a lot of times those sacrifices are monetary.

It may not have to be that much, but the sacrifice that you make, makes it possible to turn the tide in your business and in your life. You are telling the Universe, God, or Infinite ntelligence, that you are ready to take this step. You are ready to go full speed ahead without looking back. And as they say in the church, you are not putting your hand to the plow and looking back (Luke 9:62).

There is something about when you go into business for yourself that you become responsible. You are responsible for everything that happens in your life and other individuals' lives who you bring on your team and on this journey. When you are totally sold out for that, the Universe seems to wrap itself around you. The Universe seems to get on your team. You become a new individual.

Therefore, the people that were in your life at that time, if they don't elevate and grow, then you'll have to find a new family, new team members, and new individuals that will move on the same wavelength and frequency as you do. This is also a hurtful time because you love these individuals and you wanted them there. You saw them in your dreams. You know how sometimes you have dreams and you can't see everyone's faces, you can only imagine that that's your best friend.

You may see the woman you married, and that's fine, or your parents in the dream, cheering you on. The reality is that this might end up being pseudo parents or mentors that's cheering you on. It could quite possibly be, new friends. Sometimes it's a new wife or new husband that's cheering you on. And that's okay.

Let's talk about one of the biggest businesses in America, McDonald's Corporation. First and foremost, ladies and gentlemen, if you didn't know, McDonald's was started by two brothers. If you do your research, then the gentleman who joined the organization as a sales consultant to help them franchise, ended up getting the corporation from them. What's interesting about this story, is that nobody believed in him, not even his wife.

As you continue to learn more and more, you will see in his story that he divorced her and married someone else who saw his vision. Sometimes, this happens in relationships, and that's okay. What you also have to remember is that if you want to be successful, you can't allow anything or anyone to usurp the vision that you received.

You can allow people to work within it and they can get in the car with you, but they can't be negative. They can't keep hurling plan B stories and ideas at you, and they can't be trying to sabotage your vehicle as you are going in the direction to get to your destination. They must be 100% in your corner and pushing you to go forward, and giving you ideas or options to help you become successful.

The truth of the matter is when you're working a job, a lot of times you're in a position where you can take care of yourself and your family and when you become an entrepreneur, you're responsible for taking care of your employees and their families. When you are in a business and if the business is extremely successful, then the success of your business can even change the landscape of your community. This process is never talked about when we have a plan B, that's never talked about or thought about when you're making that decision.

Everybody wants safety, but I've never seen, and we've never seen this world change, with someone being safe. We've never seen greatness be achieved by somebody making a safe decision. It was always a risk involved. Now we live in a time when even your job is not safe anymore. Even with all the evidence that's been proven to us, we still believe that the job is the safest bet for a career. Starting a business with a job is the safest bet. Finishing a job before you start your business, is the worst bet.

You can start a job because you can learn all the information you need to learn about what you want to do in life. You can make connections and you can get trained, but at some point you will have to step out on your own, do what you have to do for yourself, and move out of the way. Sometimes, we time ourselves out on jobs.

When you started the job at 22, you may have started at $30,000. Now, you've been on the job for 20 years, and you're making 50 or $60,000. Let's say you retire at 70, which means that you will only be making about $75,000, if your salary continues to increase at that rate. You should have been retiring at a couple hundred grand, but you've timed yourself out. Here's what I mean.

At 22 years old, you may have started in an admin career position. Over the years, you have continued to grow in the administrative space. While you're growing in the administrative space, you also now have a 20-year old college degree. You've timed out. Now, you have a wife and kids, or husband and kids, with changed priorities. You're stuck. To your family you are everything, but to the company you're working for you're not as valuable.

There are plenty of 22 year olds fresh out of college, with fresh perspective and new ideas, that jobs are vying for. This is why going into entrepreneurship is a good idea. It breaks up the mold.

When you go out and start your own business, and you decide to go out and change the world (because that's ultimately what you're doing), you're also taking a risk and making a sacrifice.

However, in this space and time, when you make that decision to leave your job, something already told you that you can go higher and be greater. I believe that the only reason that you're leaving is because you have exhausted all other options. In order for you to get to the dream and the vision that's been placed upon you. Once you've gotten to the point of no return, there's no room for plan B. There's no room for second guessing. The only thing that's important is the vision at hand.

Find the individuals that's willing to be in your corner for this ride. Strap up, pack a bag, and get yourself prepared for the bumps in the road because it will be a long journey, but you will get there. My advice is to be prepared for one of the greatest celebrations you'll ever have in your life.

Section Two:

Ready. Set. Fight.

EXECUTION

Round 6
The Path of Personal Development

Once you decide that you're going to go into entrepreneurship full-time, you are going to have to become a *crazy* person about personal development. Every skill that you have and some of the ones you don't have, will need to be developed because you never know which skill you're going to have to display in this space and time. When you were working your job, a typical day would look like this. You would clock-in, sit at your desk or in your cubicle, do the work that you've been hired to do, and go home.

Today, this is known as *"quiet quitting."* According to an article found on NPR.com, *"Quiet quitting is not really about quitting. It's more a philosophy for doing the bare minimum at your job."* HR professionals would use this term to describe the person who has lost the motivation and momentum on the job. Nowadays, in these times, people even go *into* jobs with this attitude.

I am sure there were some special employees on your job who may have decided to stay longer, help out their fellow employees, or do a little bit more than what was required of them. Then there were others who would *always* do way more, including showing up at the job, and performing consistently at a high level every time. The truth of the matter is that out of every 100 employees, the probability of finding employees like this is around 10% or 10 individuals.

You leaving your job, meant that you probably were not one of the 10%. More than likely, you were one of the ones who went to work and did just enough to say you're doing what you say you are going to do, fulfilling your obligation, and then going home. This is especially true if you were already working on your business.

If your business was successful enough for you to think about leaving your job, then that means you devoted enough time to it after you got off work. And you probably were thinking about it while you were at work. Not only is making the choice to leave your job tough, but doing the bare minimum while you were there, indicates that you need to develop yourself more.

I am of the belief that it takes an entrepreneurial mindset to be a great employee. If you didn't possess those skills on your job, it is time to start building up the skills that you don't have. Now, granted this is not the same topic that we discussed in previous chapters, with being someone else and not being authentic. Here, we are talking about developing managerial skills.

I always say the number one characteristic of every entrepreneur is flexibility. You will find that being your own boss, will not present the same daily routine as you had on your job. The daily work was assigned for you, but as You, Inc., you will have to create your day-to-day tasks. This is why flexibility is so important. When it comes to personal development, this is about understanding what being a boss is and what true entrepreneur leadership skills are.

Remember, a lot of business owners weren't leaders in their previous position on their job. As a boss/business owner, allow me to prepare you for the rude awakening that you're going to have as you go from employee to employer. I've been around a lot of individuals in my time that have made this transition. In fact, I know several in the trucking industry, so, I'll start there.

I know and have met plenty of individuals who have driven trucks for a living. At the same time, these same individuals would talk so bad about their brokers, or the owners, of their companies. When the time came for them to move from being in the truck to being one of the owners they talked about, their tune changed. This is what you're going to encounter. Everything you thought about your boss, you are now going to want to receive sympathy and empathy from your employees because you understand what they were going through.

You're now going to understand the risks that they had to take. As the boss or owner, you will now have to manage certain aspects of the business, you never had to worry about before. Going forward, anything that's needed for your company, you and your staff are going to have to create it. There is no blueprint for you to follow or standard operating procedures for you to refer to. It's all on you. When it's time for you to create a health plan for your company, you are going to have to create it and if you don't create it, you have to be one to orchestrate it. Or, hire the people so that they can create an optimal health plan for you.

In addition to orchestrating health plans, you are also going to have to be the janitor of that new building. Not only will you have to be the janitor, but you will have to be the administrative assistant as well, until you can put someone in that position to do the job for you. This brings me back to the original point of this chapter - making this move will require training. I'm not saying that you need to learn how to be the best admin person, but it is important to have a mindset shift. One of my recommendations for this is coaching.

When you go full-time into the entrepreneurial space and you start to take leadership classes and training this can also be the place where you will potentially find your coach. This is also going to be where you're going to potentially find the individuals that are having the same experience as you are being a new entrepreneur/owner. Within these leadership classes is where you'll also find your tribe. You're going to want to go to as many classes as you can afford to attend. If necessary, then start by attending free webinars so that you can meet individuals on the same path as you. Who is dealing with the same issues as you are dealing with or finding your potential coach in that space.

Now we are living in a time where you can be a student of YouTube University and that works just fine. It's okay to start off participating in free events, but you can't remain there. YouTubers, those who have channels devoted to personal or leadership development, are able to serve as pseudo mentors or coaches. While learning from them through their platform is great, it doesn't beat having a coach to call your own. It doesn't beat being able to get on the phone with someone when you're in the thick of a deal you're trying to make or in the thick of a new transition in your company.

It's vitally important to have someone who can actually help and guide you through these challenging times in your business. Most importantly, you should be growing as you're getting this information because when you find your coach, that coach should also be busy as well in his or her business. Once you have found your coach, and they have helped you past a certain level, it is also important to note that you can't use them for the next three to five years. You should always be growing. The problems you had in year one, you shouldn't still be having in year four. Your coach should be chosen based on the timeframe you've been in business, and who can guide you on your level of development.

Take it from me, as your business grows, your problems get bigger, and as a result, the coaches you choose should be operating at a higher level. Once you receive the coaching at a higher level, you should then be in a position to be able to handle the level of business challenges that you're encountering.

The personal development phase is vital to entrepreneurs. The reason personal development is vital is because a lot of times when we jump out, we have no choice but to concern ourselves with a lot, primarily the business part. A lot of people use the phrase you're working in your business and not on your business, but they leave out the part where you are not working on yourself.

The primary concern most times is making sure our business makes money. The secondary concern is growth. We wonder why we are not growing to the levels we desire. This should concern you even if you are successful enough to create a six figure company. In order to get to that point, you have probably been working 18 hour days. No matter what your concerns are, you can't do that on your own. And when you want to take it to the next level, such as taking your company from six to seven figures, you realize you don't have that many hours in the day to make this happen.

It's not a matter of getting more hours after already working 18 hour days. Now you're trying to work the entire 24 hours, and you can't, so your mindset has to shift. As an entrepreneur, it is important to work smarter, not harder, and still make the same amount of money or more without putting in the same amount of time.

The only way this can happen is through personal development. It can only happen when you sharpen your mind. If you are working that hard in your business, then it is going to be hard to see where the shifts need to happen and when they need to come. Think about a prize fighter, Floyd

Mayweather, Oscar de la Hoya, or Manny Pacquaio's of the world. They always have someone in their corner to tell them what's going on, what they are seeing outside of the fight. The reason having someone in your corner is so important is because when you're fighting, you can't see everything because you're dodging blows and trying to throw punches. When someone else can say to you, every time you swing your right hand, you're dropping your left.

The fighter is so focused on the fight, he doesn't even realize that's a habit, but they do because they are in your corner and it's their job to watch out for you. While he will make the adjustment during the fight, it will also now become a part of his development. He knows what to work on and what to watch out for. It is the same with you, as your business is growing, your weaknesses will become known and you will know the areas of your business that needs additional development and work. Once you develop those areas, it makes it easier and so will your transition.

Hell, you might even win the fight. We tend to skip out on the area of personal development because we are so excited about making some money. We don't realize that the greatest investment we can make into our business is to make sure that *we* are better. As the CEO, we have to have a better mindset, a better understanding, and continuously stay up on the latest and greatest of our industry. Because the world keeps evolving, whatever industry your business is in, is changing rapidly everyday. If you don't know what's going on in your industry, and the latest trends, there is something wrong with that.

Most professionals have continuing education training at least annually. It is important that you participate in these training sessions because you have to stay up on current events and what's trending. Let's say you're in the technology industry or work closely with software. If you start your business and go into it working on outdated software or doing things the way they were done 30 years ago or only did it the way that you did it on your job, then you are going to be working with outdated information, making it difficult for you to be able to move and be a strong competitor in the marketplace. This is also personal development.

As we move on to subsequent chapters in the book, we will be discussing adding people to your team. If you don't know the right information and if you're not up on the latest and greatest in your area of expertise, you won't be able to put the right team in place and put them in the proper position so that you can win. Personal development cannot be overlooked.

I hope that after reading this chapter, you will understand how important it is to grow as your business grows. This is in your knowledge base because you are continuing to get lots of valuable information, which means you are pouring into your tribe as well as the coach that you will be sharing with. If you're able to do this on a continual basis, then you are moving on the right path.

Round 7
Hiring Employees

One of the funniest times in business as well as the loneliest times in business is going from employee to employer. In the previous chapter, I gave an example of people I know in the trucking industry. One of those individuals is a friend of mine. He went from being a trucker to owning his own trucking company. He had a completely different idea once he made that dramatic shift in how he looked at the brokers differently. He looked at the other owners that he worked for differently, especially when he had to take on that job and that position.

I promise you it's tough and lonely. As an employee, you and your fellow co-workers would gather around the water cooler, or you would sit in the break room together and everyone had something to talk about. This is whether you are talking about the football game that happened this past weekend. Or, you maybe showing baby pictures. Now, as the employer, you are excluded from 95% of those conversations.

Now, you don't know if those conversations are about you. People you used to hang around and would share with, now they don't want you to know about their leisure activities because you might look at them differently now that you're not one of them.

Some of your employees you'll never get to know fully. Now when you hire them, it truly becomes a work relationship at that point. I say this because a lot of people will tell you once you're doing the thing that you love, it no longer feels like work. I would venture to say that this is coming from somebody who doesn't have employees.

Once you hire employees, the real work begins. Not only are you managing a business, but you're managing different temperaments. You're managing different mindsets, and different sets of expectations. Everybody wants something different out of the job. What's interesting is that this could have always been the case, but you didn't know that because you were right there with them. I caution you to not think for one second that everybody's 100% for the team.

They understand the concept of a team, but it's not all team all the time. Some of your staff are only going to be there for a paycheck. Some are there for a paycheck *and* they want to do good work. Some are there for a paycheck, they want to do good work, and they want to learn. If you hadn't noticed the pattern yet, then you can see that the only constant is the paycheck.

They're there for the paycheck and whatever else they decide. It all depends on the individual. Everybody is different. As an employer, you will have three different categories of people who will work for you. The first type is the person who doesn't really need the job, but they're there to say that they have one, and to make some extra money.

What's most interesting is that he or she is not shy about telling people that they don't have to work here. They will say, I don't need this. Take the housewife whose husband makes a hefty six figure salary. She's going to tell you, or tell her constituents, and it will get back to you how much she doesn't need to work there.

The second type of person is the kid fresh out of college with a rich family. He will say, I don't need to work here. For all intents and purposes, he doesn't because financially he doesn't need the money. The third type is the person who has a lot of bills and who has trouble finding a better job. They may be at your company and have no plans for being there that long. But you need them for the short period of time that you will have them. You keep hearing that they're going to be leaving at any moment.

I dealt with every type of personality you can think of, when I had my cleaning business. I employed college students who didn't take the job seriously. I had formerly incarcerated individuals who because of their background couldn't get another job, and they didn't respect the job. Or, the individual who needed to borrow money against thier paycheck weekly before payday. As an employer, this is what you have to manage and deal with on a day-to-day basis. In addition to managing the different temperaments towards the job, you will also have to deal with the fact that you might not have these people working for you in 30, 60, or 90 days.

You may be wondering to yourself how do you plan? How do you make a real plan to crush the quarter if you might not have the same team by the end of it? How do you plan on crushing the year when if it keeps going this way, you'll have a new team every quarter.

Worrying about crushing the quarter and doing well in your business, can often be clouded by the fact, that your employees have their own disposition. Some people have their own qualms about them, while others, as I mentioned earlier, have families that mean more to them than your company. Your company is everything to *you*, but to them, this is just something to do for eight hours. You have to manage that.

Now, there is one other important factor I want to call to your attention. That is, in addition to having trouble on your job, with your employees, you will also have no friends. You will especially have no friends on the job and it will seem as if everybody's against you. Of course, everybody's with you as long as you're paying them, and as long as you are doing what you say you're going to do for them. However, it's going to be very tough to find employees who will be on your side.

Despite the evidence from reading an article on Google or watching a video on YouTube, if they paid attention, they will realize that people that have businesses are not always the richest people in the world. For some reason, every employee has decided to believe that if you are the boss, you are making all of the money. The opposite is true. There's actually proven statistics that some companies have started where the employees are making more money than the boss. It might not stay that way, but there are times and certain instances when that happens. This knowledge doesn't seem to trickle down to the employees.

The employees believe that not only do you make all the money, but you have it all. And because of this, you can always afford to pay them more. In their minds, you have no other expenses. It is ironic, that they've never taken into account what it costs for you to run the business or provide apparatuses for them to work, so that they can provide for themselves and their families. Sound lonely? It is!

Let me give my married couples some advice. I hope that you got everything sorted out in the beginning phases of the business because you are going to need each other. If you are doing well enough in your business, financially, to hire multiple individuals, then you should actually have a good thing going on at this point. If you have a supportive spouse, I pray that you can lean on him or her because this will be the first person I would recommend you to talk to and have in your corner. Your spouse will be your safe haven when you're coming in from facing the cold world.

When you walk into the door after a long day, and close it to the outside world, it should be a blessing to be able to have somebody you can unload on, not to the point of their detriment, but to a point of your relief. This makes it possible for you to be able to say, Hey, this is what I've had to deal with today. These were the issues that occured at work. I'm dealing with it the best way I know how, but what do you think I should do?

In a perfect world, you'll have that man or that woman in your corner, at this particular time, in your business, especially when you've reached the point of hiring employees. If you're not married, then you definitely should be able to lean on your tribe. This is why I said in the previous chapter that you have to go all in on personal development and attend opportunities for education and training. The people you are going to see, are the people who are dealing with the same issues and having the same struggles that you are dealing with right now.

It would be great if you all could join together and create a mastermind. A group where you guys can go golfing, or bowling and have some discussion about your challenges, so that you're not dealing with them alone. This can be a lonely time because the people you thought you had in your corner, you have discovered that they do not care about your business the way you would like or want them to. My question to you is why should they?

It's not their business. It's yours. When you understand that, you can bring them the same level of energy that they bring you. Not negative, but matching whatever energy needs to be matched at the time so that you can get through and still be able to successfully steer the ship whether these individuals are with you or not.

I have mentioned the importance of having a tribe throughout the book, but if you haven't yet created one, it is important to develop it. Your tribe should be filled with other individuals that are striving to be successful business owners like you are. They don't have to be your personal friends, but you definitely have to put yourself in a situation where you're spending a significant amount of time with them. And when I say significant, I'm talking a couple of times a month face to face and at least once a week in conversation on a telephone.

Sometimes you can get the help you need and information on how to fix your issue without even having to completely divulge the problem you're going through or be in this place where you are comfortable being able to air out what's going on and have somebody being able to give you the advice you need.

Also, put yourself around coaches. The greatest people in the world have coaches. They have coaches to help them at each level. The coach you have for the last level is not the coach to take you to the next level. Get a new coach. Maybe you need a coach for leadership and not just a regular business coach. Maybe you need a life coach. Maybe you need a wellness coach because physically the business is wearing you out. And now you find yourself needing more stamina.

Maybe you need to get your health together, to be able to deal with this portion of the fight. Make no mistake, you are in the middle of the fight of your life right now. You are pretty much going towards the end of the fight, now that we are in round seven. This portion of the fight requires more energy, and more stamina than you thought you would have needed to get you through this portion. Without the energy and the stamina you are already doomed, risking not only being worn out, but being knocked out.

This moment is when those in your corner shines the brightest. This is where the training that you have had shines the brightest and shows up the best. This is where your eating habits, and your physical routine show themselves to be true. This is the part of the business where you'll really begin to see it flourish. For example, when you practice by yourself, you don't know if you have it until you bring other people in the ring with you.

And when you hire your employees, that's when the fight starts. You've been practicing, you've been working hard, but when you allow other people to get in, you truly become an entrepreneur then because you're not only responsible for your health and wellbeing and how you make money, but you're responsible for a dozen other households and you have to be in a different mindset, in a different space, and in different shape to be able to do that successfully. And no matter what, remember, you can't do it alone.

Round 8
Reinvesting

Round 8 brings me to my favorite part of business, reinvesting. Full disclosure, it wasn't always my favorite part of the business experience, or this entrepreneurial fight, as I am calling it. When talking about reinvestment, the first thing that comes to mind is the time when I had my cleaning business. When I was in my 20s, I started a commercial cleaning business and I was told by people who I absolutely hated that I needed to reinvest. I didn't hate them personally because I didn't know them personally, but from a business perspective, I hated them. I later realized that they were helping me or at least attempting to help me properly run a business.

In their process of helping me, they were very aggravating. Me being young and in my twenties, I didn't want to hear it and I didn't understand that great advice can come from people that you don't particularly like. This is a lesson that I should have remembered from school, especially when it came to teachers. It seemed like it was the teacher's job to aggravate us, so we accepted that from them.

However, when you're doing phenomenal work and you're performing at a high level, you don't expect for them to still yell at you. You don't expect for people to still have something to complain about. The complaints and yelling I received were people that I worked with on a contract for my cleaning business. They saw me growing in the space and they just kept giving me advice. One thing that always stood out to me is one of them telling me that I have to reinvest my money.

They saw that I was making money and enjoying myself. I had bought a new car, and did plenty of shopping, but they were constantly in my ear, saying make sure you reinvest your money and put it back into the business. Well, I didn't take their advice. I did the exact opposite, long story short. Looking back at it now, I knew I would've had a seven figure plus business if I would've listened.

Reinvestment is the single easiest way to grow your business exponentially, but it's a hard thing to do. Why is that? At this point, you've read through seven chapters of *Business Corner*, hearing me tell you how hard it is to do business. I've given you examples of times when you are going to be alone running your business. You have read about people walking out on you, you have read about spouses being upset with you. Now you find yourself in a space in your business, where you're actually making money, and the business is working.

Maybe your spouse left, but he or she came back. Maybe you're making new friends, and finally getting your head above water and you're able to breathe. Once you are able to catch your breath, you have a decision to make. Am I comfortable here or do I want my business to grow? If you are a true entrepreneur, then you're going to choose option B. You're going to want the business to grow.

Maybe you are successfully bringing in a hundred plus thousand dollars a year. You've created a living for yourself. You're doing the things that you need to do. You're past the point of surviving, now you're thriving, but the business is your baby. And your baby is in your house until they're 18, well, in most houses. And now they want to go out and explore. That's your business. You have to let that business go out and have a life of its own. You may be asking yourself, how do you make that happen?

Just like you invest in college for your child, you have to reinvest in that business. You have to take that extra 20, 30, 40, or $50,000 that you've saved up or earned in profits and put it back into the business. Yes, it sounds crazy. It's going to sound crazy to your spouse because they probably have access to looking at the bank accounts and are going to see you take all of that money and reinvest it. While simultaneously, they are going to think of all the trips, vacations, new purses or cars that you could have bought with that money.

Instead, you went and got a new office space, purchased new equipment, or hired different individuals. You did all of these things for your company and that's tough. And where do you find yourself? Right back in a space by yourself because nobody that's around you, except for the coaches that we talked about previously, and the people who should still be in your corner, your peers and the people that you set up, is going to understand this move. The tricky part about the business is even though you have these individuals in your corner at that time, you're not doing it for them. You're not doing it for their love, and for their approval. You're not doing it to take care of them or provide for them. It's usually the people that you are doing it for that are the ones that don't understand, or they understand the least.

What's even more sad is that they don't try to understand, and get more knowledge and understanding so that they can be right there with you. The ones that do, they are anomalies. Here you find yourself making another crazy decision in their mind and you have to think and ask yourself the question, am I really crazy? No, you're an entrepreneur. You want this business to grow. You want this business to be something bigger than you. You want this business to be something that the world looks at as something great, and not just how you make money.

This is when your business starts to have something called a *valuation.* A valuation is where people can understand that your business can stand alone without you and that it's actually worth something outside of the work that you put in. This is how you start to take your business into the home stretch. This is how you take your business from surviving to thriving.

Maybe you went from surviving to thriving by the money that you're earning from the business, but now the business has to go out like that kid and learn how to survive on its own. It's going to take your resources, it's going to take your savings, and it's going to take your support to push it out there. Allow other individuals to take your place, and invest in the tools and apparatuses for the business to do its thing successfully without you full time.

It is a hard decision as I stated, but if you want your business to be great, you will make this decision.

Now, yes, I think that you can live off of the fact that you've defied the odds thus far. Those individuals that you might have disappointed for a short period of time, now they can see that you have a leg to stand on. You can say, *"Hey, I have gotten us out of the fire before."* At this point because you've probably gotten out of 10 fires and they should have some type of faith in you. You should try to have some type of faith in yourself to lean on when you're trying to explain to your wife or your friends or anybody else you're trying to tell, to go with you on this path. We got through it before, we can get through it again.

The business is making money. The business is its own entity. Before it was an idea, and now it is an actual thing. You have that to rest on, but you still have to continue to lean on those individuals that should be in your corner at that time because they're the ones that's going to be giving you the positive information. They're the ones that's going to be telling you positive thoughts when you are hearing all the negative. There is one new person that you have to add to your vision, team, and corner. This person has to be a visionary.

A lot of times those individuals can tell you their thoughts and ideas from their experience and their vision, but at this point in your business, somebody has to step up and be a visionary that's only focused on *your* vision. They can take your vision, continue to move it forward to higher heights, and create a vision within your vision. Sometimes this person is your wife or your husband because they've seen enough, now, they believe. Sometimes it's an employee that you brought on that's been along for the ride and they're willing to bet everything on you.

Whoever that person is, that's the new person that needs to be added to your corner and it's function of your business because it's not for you to be the only person casting the vision and seeing it through. This is not only for you to see it through. This is for you to put someone in place for them to take it to the next level. You did what you were supposed to do, and that is you brought it this far.

This next phase is not for you to go alone. This is not for people to be on the sideline. This next phase is not just about the people that's in your corner, this next phase is for the people that's actually going to be their and fight with you. The fight is now bigger than ever before. Before when you were fighting, it was one on one and now it'll be two or three on one and you cannot be in that ring swinging by yourself.

For my WWF or WWE fans, this is a tag team match. For some people's businesses it would be a Battle Royale or a Royal Rumble. Make sure that the people that are in the ring with you during this portion of the fight knows your vision, are sold on your vision and willing to create their vision within yours, so that you can go as far as your company needs to go.

Round 9
Relocation

If you have ever taken an organized business class, such as Business 101 that they offer in college, one of the beginning principles you'll be taught in class, is location, location, location. What this means is that the location of your business is just as, if not more important, than the business itself. I always like to use the example of selling surfboards. If you want to own a business selling surfboards, then it makes sense to move to the beach because, selling surfboards in the desert for example, might not be the greatest idea.

You may be saying, but Jay we live in the world of technology. We live in a time where you can sell products online and via social media. Because of this most businesses and business owners don't put a lot of emphasis on that old adage of *location, location, location.* This is especially true for small and micro business owners in this country. The classification of a small/micro business means that you make less than $500 million dollars in annual revenue. Considering this classification, there are a lot of small business owners, that are not really thinking about that.

When you reach the point of reinvesting in your business, it means that you have reached a point of making your company bigger than it was. It means that you've put all your profits back into your business because you made the decision that you weren't going to turn back. It means that you knew you and your company were ready to go into the next stage of growth in your business. During this time, we have our team with us, we have the vision, we have the sub-visionaries, the people that are running with us to bring the vision to pass, and people who have now created their own vision within yours.

Reinvesting in your business, means that you are moving up and onward to higher and greater heights. Because of this, you're usually in the space mentally where you realize something has to change and a lot of times it is your location. Relocation is a part of business that many business owners don't talk about. The thought of moving not only you, but your family, along with your business, can be overwhelming. Let me also state that relocation doesn't always mean you have to be moving to a new city or state.

Sometimes it can mean physically moving, but other times this might mean taking your business outside of the house, or your garage, and moving your meetings from Starbucks or Panera Bread, into an office space. The growth of your business has now reached the point of dictating your location. This is a fun time and it can also be a stressful time because the concern can grow to am I going too far? Am I buying too much land? Am I buying too big of a building? Am I getting too much space for my office? Do I need all of this space and many other questions that may plague your mind.

It is important to pay close attention to the business itself and not only you. Your business is likened to the child I mentioned in the previous chapter. When it becomes time to let your child go and off into the real world, we like to try and steer them into the college or career that we want to steer them in. And we are not paying attention to what they like, talents they exhibit, or strengths they've already displayed in front of us. Most times, our children are showing us what they're naturally talented and gifted at doing.

We become focused and overbearing parents worried about what we want for our children. As a result, our children rebel and your business can do the same exact thing, which is why you have to pay close attention to the business as a completely separate entity. As an overbearing parent, you can mess up before your business goes to the stratosphere that you saw in your vision.

This is one specific time in your business when you need outside influence. You need to have someone in your corner that can provide you with a critique of your business at this point. The mention of the word critique can make anyone nervous. Critique scares people, but your business is already an entity. It has already made a footprint in the local community that it is in. It's not going to falter because somebody offered a critique of your business and/or pointed out a few faults. The moment of critique is the moment when your business gets stronger. You have to treat your business like a living and breathing organism.

That constructive criticism is going to build you. It's going to build your company, it's going to build your organization and it is going to make sure that you are able to cross all the T's and dot all the I's. Sometimes in that critique, someone's going to tell you something that you never expected to hear, and it's going to be that you need to relocate. You're going to say, *"What?! I'm doing great here. The last five years I've been in the black. I'm doing well. I've reinvested a hundred thousand dollars into my company and we are great. We're ready to go knock it out or the park, and take over."* We have a hard time separating ourselves, and leaving things behind that's good so that we can go for the great. What you have to understand is that your business is not built for one place. Some of the greatest companies in this world started in the place that they are. The next thing you know, they're business is in every city in the country, or different cities in one region, or multiple cities in your state.

You have to be willing, have the flexibility, and the open-mindedness in order to be able to let your business flourish and grow to the greatest heights that it can. Sometimes the biggest obstacle that's holding you back outside of yourself is the location. Sometimes, we are okay being a big fish in the small pond, and while that maybe okay for you, it's not okay for your business.

As I grew in business in the state of South Carolina, especially when the Pandemic hit, I started to travel. After the world opened back up, I was traveling to different parts of the country and I realized that the things I learned in South Carolina, they didn't know in California, Las Vegas, and parts of Arizona, even though they are bigger cities.

Bigger cities, didn't mean they had the same resources. What I did find out is that those individuals on the Westside of the country, were way more willing to purchase the product and services that my company had to offer as opposed to those in South Carolina. Even though I was able to do well in South Carolina, it was always like pulling teeth. I had to sell, oversell, and sell again to get someone to do business as opposed to going to another place where the runway for success was greater and further. The participants were way more willing to purchase and patronize the services I had.

When you get yourself into a situation like this, you have to be willing, for your business sake, to relocate. I would not have been able to do that without the right conversations, right people, and right guidance from the people who wanted to see me thrive and succeed with my business where I was. There were a few things that could not be denied. What could never be denied is the numbers. They could not deny the opportunities, and they supported and laid the groundwork so that it could be an amazing transition. These are the people that you need to have in your corner. Everybody's going to say to you, *"Oh, you're doing good here, you're doing great here. You're doing good here and that's fine, but are you great?"* And the question you have to ask yourself is, am I willing to give up the good to go to the great?

The person making six figures, and making a living for themselves had to make a decision that they wanted to give up whatever the work ethic and the formula was that was working, to adopt a new formula to make seven figures. It was working, but it's not going to get you to where you want to go next. I always like to use the analogy that when you're climbing the ladder to success and you get to a certain level, whatever you had at that level, you can't put on your back and carry it to the next one.

You have to be willing to leave the larger items behind. Take the small bits and pieces that you can fit in your backpack and take it to the next level. The six figure level is for somebody else, and reigning supreme in a small town is for somebody else. At the time, you were fluorishing in a 500 square foot office. Now, it's time for you to go to that 3,000 or 5,000 square foot office. The 500 square foot office is for somebody else. You've done that and you don't want to time yourself out in that space because there's another hungry person doing the same thing you are doing. The person that is hungry is coming and they're taking cheaper prices than you are. They are willing to cut corners.

Then again, people are finicky. They will do business with someone for 30 years and then say to themselves and you, that they are going to give someone else a shot. This is in spite of the relationship you've built with them and the quality of work you've provided. These should all be signs for you to move on, matriculate, and get to the place where you are supposed to be. Let's describe it in another way, and look at pyramids.

Pyramids are often used in a negative analogy. For example, think about the feeling you get when someone mentions a pyramid scheme. You may put a frown on your face or turn up your nose. However, a pyramid itself is a majestic creation. When we are using certain words as descriptors, we don't think of how great they are. A pyramid is amazing when it's built.

In fact, pyramids are a great wonder of the world. However, when you are in a pyramid, while it's being formed, you have an opportunity to get in where you fit in. At the same time, when you're being built, you can go to the top if you have what it takes. With the stamina, physical, and mental wellness that we mentioned in the previous chapter.

In this space and time, you are building something. Yes, there will come a time when you are building your business and it will hit that apex. We'll dive more into this in the upcoming chapter. Until you reach that apex, you're still building your pyramid, you're still building this amazing monument in your business. And it's not for you to stay at the bottom. It's not for you to stay in the middle. Don't get comfortable because your goal is to get to the top. Maybe the only way for you to get to the top, is to reconcile within yourself that you are going to have to move. And you will have to keep moving before you get stuck.

When you get to that level of business, and the numbers are right, what happened is that everything is pointing up and is signaling in the direction that you want to go in order to give up the good and go to the great. This also means that you have placed those individuals in your corner at that time that can coach and advise you, and see past your love for where you are. Your love for that six figure space or seven figure space that you've been resting in for the last few years.

I believe that you don't want to rest there, I believe that you want to take your business and allow it to go to the heights that it has the potential to. Wrap your mind around the fact, that this may end up in relocation. Unfortunately, once you reach a certain level or plateau in your business, you're not going to have another choice. You're going to have to choose to relocate. You will come to realize that this place will be better for your business.

This past year we saw one of the richest men in the world, well, at the time this book is being written he is one of the richest men in the world, Elon Musk move from California to Austin, Texas. This is important to note because even a billionaire realized that although he can live in California and he would be fine, his business was going to suffer there. One because the prices were too high in California and his business wasn't going to perform at its best. He had a good thing going. He built Tesla, and Paypal in California. In spite of these successes, he had to feel as though his business could be greater moving to Austin.

If he can benefit from relocation at that point in his business, we have to consider this in our small businesses. We might need to think heavy about relocation, making sure that we have the same type of individuals that he must have had in his corner to counsel and guide him to make that decision and to take his business from as great as it was and put it in position to be greater.

Round 10

Closing the Book on Your Business

My very first gift as an entrepreneur was a book called, *How to Value and Sell Your Business*. The premise of this book is The Essential Guide to Preparing, Valuing, and Selling a Company for Maximum Profit. Now, at 25 years old, I hadn't the slightest idea what they were talking about. I realized that a lot of people are in the same boat, especially now with the invention of social media. Most people are talking about business from the perspective of what you can do to make money. This is the wrong way to think about business.

At this point in the book, I've written several chapters and I have emphasized how important it is to keep the business separate from you. Not only did I emphasize this, but I gave examples such as your business being like your child. We talked about the stages of growth of your child and at this point in the process, you have to let that child go.

You have to let that child go so that it can have its own life. Just because you're letting the child go, doesn't mean you aren't connected to them. You're forever connected to your child. Your child is going to show traits that you've imparted in him or her, traits that they inherently have from you not only because they've been around you, but also because they have your DNA in them. Whatsoever the case may be, your child is still independent of you. It has to be. And so once you take the necessary steps to make your business independent from you, the conversation about the end goal has to come up. In *Business Corner,* we are not talking about being self-employed we are disspelling the myth that they're one and the same. In my opinion, you are either an entrepreneur or you're self-employed. Being self-employed can be where you start. Honestly, it's where most people start. If you really and truly want to be an entrepreneur, then you're going to have to take this a step further and put your business out there on its own, and allow it to thrive and flourish without you having your hands on every single part of it. Without it even focusing on you.

Let's think of the greats. One of the biggest companies that we have now and that ever has been is *Microsoft*. A lot of people may be surprised to know that it's been years now since its founder, Bill Gates is no longer the CEO.

Now, he's just a shareholder. Even though he doesn't make most of the company decisions anymore, Microsoft is going to be forever synonymous with him. However, Microsoft continues day to day and he has almost nothing to do with it. Steve Jobs, co-founder of *Apple* has passed away, and has been for several years now. He does not run the day-to-day operations of Apple. Apple is still going without him. Sam Walton, the founder of Walmart, is no longer here. Walmart is still going on and even the children of Mr. Walton are only mere shareholders.

They're not running the day to day operation of this corporation. You, fellow business owner, has to start practicing and being like the people who are successful in business. Success leaves clues. Some of us are steadilytrying to start our businesses in the dark and figure it out on our own, when there's plenty of light around us to be had.

When this gentleman gave me the book so many years ago, again I didn't know anything about it. However, as the years went on, I understood it. More importantly, when I was forced to sell my business because of the housing crisis that went on between the years of 2008 and 2012, I got a rude awakening. I was able to fully understand what this book meant because my company did have a valuation and I was able to sell it for some money.

If I was working my business for this, I could have sold it for 10 times more. If I was planning and evaluating my business and preparing it for maximum profit, then I could have sold it for more. This is why I thought that this would be an amazing topic to go through, once I started talking about *Business Corner*. The goal of this book was for us to go through all phases of your business cycle and real businesses are sold every single day.

If you go on *Craigslist* or on *Google* for example, and type "Businesses for

Sale," in the search bar, you can put in your local city and you'll see that a lot of businesses for sale every day. This is an entirely different world that most entrepreneurs don't talk about. And I wanted to make sure we talked about it here because it is an important subject. People are not starting businesses from scratch as much as you think they are. A lot of people are buying existing businesses because the entrepreneur who started the business might not be the entrepreneur to take the business to the next level for the next 30 or 40 years.

It might have to change three or four hands before that happens within that 30, 40 year timeframe. This is what's called a business cycle. And there's nothing crazy about it. Your job is to do what you are meant to do with it. Make it great.

Follow this process, value, prepare, and sell that company for maximum profit. How do you do this? As we have discussed continuously throughout the book, you have to have the proper people in your corner at this time of your business. One of the reasons is because emotions are running high. These emotions don't have to be negative. These emotions can be great because this is your baby. You started it from scratch. You will say to yourself, I remember being in my garage or sitting on my computer in my living room. I remember my son or my daughter being right there helping me out and now I'm thinking about selling. It can and it should bring tears to your eyes

The business could have also been painful to you in the last 10 years and now you actually have an opportunity to sell it. You're like, "Yes!" or, you can be like most entrepreneurs who start their businesses and don't have this in mind at all. This is where it gets emotional for me because we are missing out on a grand opportunity. We have to continue to matriculate through parts of our lives and we don't have to be attached to something like the proverbial ball and chain is attached to your leg.

You can have a business for five and 10 years or more, grow it, make it profitable, sell it to somebody else, *and* go on to something greater. Many people in life start something in their twenties and they feel as if they're stuck. By the time they're 30 or 40 years old, they feel as though because they lost so much time, they can't try the next thing and the next thing. Too much time has passed and they feel that there is no room for them to start over. Some people around them may feel as if they aren't doing well because they're not doing the same thing as when they started. We have to get past this belief. Selling a business is normal.

You may be wondering, What goes into this? Who do I turn to? I'm glad you asked. The first person that needs to be in your corner at this time is the person that came on with you in the last chapter. The person who decided that they want to partner with you and take on your vision. I say this because they're going to be the people that are going to benefit the most. Or, they are going to be the people most affected because a lot of times they've adopted your vision for the company. They brought into that, but they didn't ever see you selling the company or them leaving the company.

When you start to talk about selling it or think about selling it and they don't have that in their vision, you can create a real bad situation for you and your company. You can create bad blood, and they can stop producing like they once were, so now, even if you do sell because of their lack of work ethic, they can bring the valuation of the company down. There are so many things that can happen because of their actions or inaction. This is because they are the ones that know everything.

They know where all the bodies are buried. They know how you make your money. They know where the strengths, weaknesses, opportunities, and threats are. For my beginner business owners, this is what's known as the *SWOT Analysis*. They know the business inside and out. It is very important for you to make sure that they're still in your corner at this point in your business. My advice is to have this conversation with them in advance. Start showing them the benefits of selling and the future possibilities of what can happen if the business is sold.

My next piece of advice is to offer them the business if you really want to sell it because not only are they sold out for it, they've also bought into the business at this point. This is their baby too, their adopted baby, but baby nonetheless. They've been in the trenches with you for the last five or 10 years. Their families count on this business as well. Put them in position to have first write of refusal, get their input, find out how they feel about it, and see if this is something that they want to do. This can be the easiest transition. If you can sell a business to these individuals that you have already been working alongside of, then you'll feel better at the end of the day. You know the business is in good hands and with people you know. If you wanted to, then you could still pop in and give advice on anything they may be dealing with.

It's hard for us entrepreneurs to ever give up the business. LOL. As long as you don't close the door to us, we are definitely going to keep coming back to give our advice. My point is that the transition is 10 times smoother, if you can sell the business to someone who is already in it.

A lot of people, if they are successful, may choose to take their business public. Now you need to bring in the "big dogs." I'm not only talking about coaches here. If you want to take your business public, then you need to bring big consultants into your space. People who are used to navigating the space of taking companies public. You will also need to have better attorneys, and forensic accountants. All of these major people are now no longer in your corner. Their relationship with you had to change. They are now on your team so that the transition can happen properly. This is a great step.

This means that you've done a monumental job as an entrepreneur running your company if you have the opportunity to take it public. Let me caution you, a lot of hiccups can happen in the process of going from private to public. Having the right team is pivotal. No expense needs to be spared on having the right individuals. Let me repeat the list of who you will need, lawyers, accountants, and consultants that have the successful history of taking a company from private to public on your team during this process. The last option, which can be good or bad depending upon the state of the company, is you selling it outright to whoever wants to buy it. This means that you're putting it out on the open market.

Sometimes in business, you may feel as if you've gone as far as you can go with it and you are in a space in your life, where you want to do something different. That's totally fine. We have to be okay with that. We have to know when we have pushed our limit. If that's the case, then when it comes to the people you need, make sure your spouse is on board. If you can, make sure that everybody that's on your team will be taken care of or at least have the expectation that they'll be taken care of to the extent that they're okay or they can have the opportunity to leave the job so you don't put anybody in a bad space and hurt their family.

What can happen is that when new people come into a company, sometimes they come in and break it up or they see the business differently. People can at times lose their jobs. We all know what it looks like when things are bad, so I'm not going to elaborate on that as much as I would on the other three. However, things can be going bad and as the business owner, you might want to stop the bleeding so you choose to sell the company.

Those other three are amazing opportunities and you might already have something new that you want to do. This is what business looks like, especially when you reach a certain place and for a successful business, this is the life cycle. What's missing, and what people don't talk about, is who's by your side? Who's in your corner? Who has your back through every part of the process? This is what *Business Corner* was about. This is why I decided to create this project because we have to combat the social media rhetoric that you can start a business, make a million dollars, and everything could be okay. There is so much more that goes into it.

There is a statistic that says that 80% of businesses that start don't make it through the first five years. I'm still questioning that statistic because I'm trying to figure out if they are saying that because they can't find the business in the phone book or because they don't see the business out. Or, are they checking for the company's tax return or lack thereof? I don't know what they're doing. I have to find that portion out. It is my belief that a lot of these businesses are not actual businesses.

I think that these businesses are really made up of self-employed individuals who are stepping out from their jobs, trying to do their own thing, and then once it gets too hard, they go back to work. However, if this statistic is correct, I believe that the topics covered in *Business Corner* will fix it. I'm willing to bet that 80% of individuals that lose their business, 80%, don't have people in their corner.

And if they do have people in their corner, they don't have the right people in their corner. They are not going through the process and switching out the people when they are supposed to. They are not leaning on those individuals when the time comes and they don't have a clue of the destination they want to go to. If you don't know where you are and you don't know where you want to go, then you'll never be able to find the right path to get there.

This is the reason why I created *Business Corner*, and one of the things that I want you to get out of it, is clarity on what you want to do next and guidance on the proper direction needed so that you can reach your destination.

Special Note

As a business coach, and more importantly, a veteran entrepreneur, I know how important it is to have someone in your corner. There were many times throughout my business and entrepreneurial journey, where I have not only felt alone, but I have been alone starting a business without any financial backing, and with no support from family members.

I had to learn firsthand where I would have to sacrifice the finances I could have made being the best parent I could be, while being an entrepreneur. I've been in situations where I totally compromised myself because I didn't have people in my corner, to make sure I remained truly authentic to who I am. Once I realized that I wasn't being authentic to myself, it was at that point that I dove into personal development, so that I could continue to grow as opposed to just growing my business. I've seen the direct result of how reinvesting in your business, can completely turn it around and generate more revenue than I could have ever thought possible. I've been through the phases of relocation, moving my business and my family to multiple states and back again.

Long story short, I've been where you are, no matter which round you find yourself in. Now, through this book, I am placing myself in your business corner, and allowing my experiences, knowledge, and wherewithal, to not only guide you, but equip you with what's needed so that you can survive the fight.

About J Haleem

J Haleem went from working for $8.00 an hour at the Hampton Inn, to earning six figures as a Commercial Photographer in just a few years. He was able to accomplish all this while being a convicted felon. While working for $8.00 an hour he developed his mantra #I Won't Starve, which was the catalyst for him to leave his job after only one year. Over his career, he's been able to work with international brands like Nike, Save The Children Foundation, NFL, Amtrak & The WNBA.

Since then, he has been pardoned, and is now an author and motivational speaker. J Haleem uses the #I Won't Starve message to encourage and motivate students, entrepreneurs and career-oriented individuals. His goal is to inspire you to build a platform to ensure that U Won't Starve.

Contact J Haleem

To learn more about J Haleem, or to purchase his books or brand merchandise, visit:
www.iwontstarve.com.

J Haleem is available for speaking engagements and special events. To book J Haleem, e-mail:
info@jhaleem.com.

Made in the USA
Middletown, DE
14 October 2023